Review Tales
A Book Magazine For Indie Authors

Founder & Editor in Chief: S. Jeyran Main
Publisher: Review Tales Publishing & Editing Services
Print & Distribution: Ingram Spark
Designs: Pexels
ISBN 978-1-988680-54-5 (Paperback)
ISBN 978-1-988680-55-2 (Digital)
www.jeyranmain.com
For all inquiries, please contact us directly.

Contribitors

Candace Lynn Talmadge
Emil Rem
Hawa Who
Dan Ehl
Jenna Greene
Benedict Stuart
Alexander Ellis
Fred Calvert
J. M. Shaw
Kim Lengling
Linnea Tanner
Mark Leslie
Machiel Hoek
Shama Shams
Tong Ge
Tricia Copeland
J. L. Yarrow
Lara Gelya
Mike P
Ron Root
Jennifer Anne Gordon
Cyrus A. Ansary
Patricia Skipper
Thomas Richard Spradlin
Indignus Servus
Charlie Sheldon

Photo Credits from Pexels:
Taryn Elliott- 6259449
Karolina Grabows- 5427039
Taryn Elliott - 9663106

Editor's Note

Dear Readers,

As the year turns and we settle into the cozy embrace of winter, I am delighted to welcome you to the 13th edition of our magazine. This season, we delve into the heart of storytelling with fresh insights from authors who share their tales and the sometimes strange, often surprising places those tales come from.

This issue brims with reflections on the writing journey. From the curious wells of inspiration that spark new stories to the delicate balance between vulnerability and resilience every author must hold, each article captures the spirit of creativity and determination. Our contributors also touch on the challenges and fragile moments of "literary deaths by neglect," as well as navigating the fine line that often defines our work with readers. These themes remind us how courageous it takes to be a storyteller—to pour ourselves into our words with confidence and humility.

With a new year ahead, may we all embrace the unknown with open hearts and renewed purpose. This is a time for growth, and for the writing community, it's a time to support and uplift each other as we continue to shape and share our narratives. Together, we form a community that strengthens each other's voices and provides a haven for creativity to flourish.

So, here's to a year of new chapters, endless stories, and a thriving community. May 2025 bring you inspiration, joy, and the courage to embrace your journey, wherever it leads.

Happy New Year to all, and happy reading!

Warmly,

Jeyran Main

Editor-in-Chief
Review Tales Magazine

WINTER 2025 | ISSUE 13

Contents

My Weird Source of Story Ideas for My Paranormal Fiction Series

Candace Lynn Talmadge

When I was 13, my best friend's mother put a Taylor Caldwell novel in my hand and said, "You can write one of these."

Not long before that, I had discovered The Lord of the Rings and was enchanted, reading it repeatedly.

I wanted to write a fantasy novel, but it differed from the usual quest-based tale. For decades I daydreamed on and off,. Over time many characters emerged in my thoughts. I saw them, heard them speak, and followed their lives.

I also researched arcane topics like Atlantis, which led me beyond a rabbit hole to a massive paradigm shift. Call it an appreciation for broader realities beyond the purely physical.

I also understood at long last that the multigenerational story I wanted to chronicle arose out of multiple past lives I have lived. Only then could I begin drafting the series I eventually titled Stoneslayer.

The first-generation heroine, Helen Andros (one of my past lives), lived in an island nation, Azgard, that was sharply divided between two peoples: stark income and race disparities between the ultra-rich overclass and everyone else. There is a stark divide in political power between the two camps. Cruelty for its own sake — because no one else in power would hold the wrongdoers to account.

Azgard was also a theocracy defined by sectarian dogmas. The longer I live in the United States today, the more my country resembles the one I inhabited when I lived as Helen.

The state religion of Azgard elevated one race over another and forbade sexual relationships between the two peoples. Helen was the mixed-race love child of such an unlawful union.

There were profound and devastating consequences for one of her parents and Helen once her close, hidden relationship with the highest ranked in the land became public. The mighty Temple of Kronos, the state religious institution, took a lethal interest in her.

A chaos demon seeking the power to annihilate aligned with one of the top Temple priests who wanted ultimate control in Azgard. The resulting cataclysmic rampage overturned everything and reverberated in my life down through the ages right to my current life, in which I finally turned the tables on the demon and vanquished it from my being. The tale goes on....

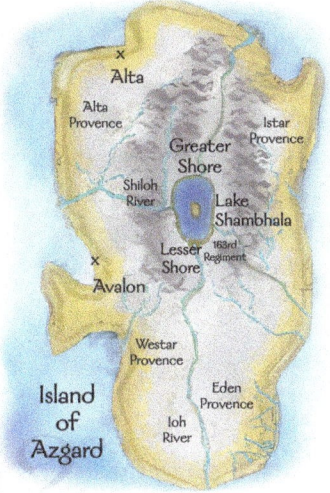

Troubles with Readers

Emil Rem

Heart of New York ("HONY") was created as a challenge. Although my previous book had received accolades galore, I remained dissatisfied. Writing is so easy because it concerns people and places I love.

"If you want to prove how good you are," I asked myself," see if you can write about a subject you dislike."

I chose a Christmas holiday in New York. My younger son persuaded the rest of my family that Christmas in the sunny Caribbean wouldn't cut it. A born-again Goth, the place to be was in Harlem in mid-winter.

The bitter, miserable, wind-blown, snow-sleet weather demoralized me completely.

My writing is about comparing and contrasting the eccentrics and landmarks of one place to another. I chose to contrast New York with….. Calgary, Canada, the Siberia of the North.

The dismal weather revealed the most dismal stories of sacrifice, manipulation, and financial downfall.

It could have gone better with the staunch fans gained by my previous book.

"Why did you neglect this colorless winter tale's sunny, humorous, intriguing travelogues? You should hang up your hat and call it a day before you publish HONY and ruin your reputation."

I kept sending these 'fans' chapter after chapter and got the same response.

Halfway through the book, I received an irate call. "That Joe character was so bad. Why did he do what he did? I would never have done that. This is what anyone in their right mind would have done." The fan ranted on for half an hour.

Fed up, I almost screamed, "If you don't like my character, why waste so much time discussing him and his actions."

It was then that the penny dropped. This book was not a sun-shiny bagatelle of amusing anecdotes. It delved into the grey borders of life and decisions forced upon us, sometimes in a flash. Which way would we jump?

Once my 'fans' understood the premise that accompanied the miserable weather in both countries, they began to detect a gentle humor and a streak of love embedded within, like a seam of gold gleaming out of a grey bed of rock.

STORIES of LOSS, REDEMPTION & FAMILY

Heart of New York

EMIL REM

03

Embracing Vulnerability: My Journey As An Author

Hawa Who

Becoming an author is more than writing—it's about embracing vulnerability and connecting with readers through authentic storytelling. I knew it would be deeply personal when I began writing Petals of My Heart. The themes of love, loss, and self-discovery are drawn from my own life, and writing became an act of self-reflection and courage.

Through poetry, I explored complex relationships, particularly with my mother, and learned that honesty in writing opens a space for others to relate.

Through poetry, I explored complex relationships, particularly with my mother, and learned that honesty in writing opens a space for others to relate. Although intimidating, vulnerability creates the most profound connections between the writer and the reader. As I wrote each poem, I uncovered more about myself and, surprisingly, found that my words resonated with others navigating their emotional landscapes.

Another important aspect of my journey is discovering my voice as a writer. I'm originally from Ghana and grew up in New York City, which gave me a unique lens through which I see the world. This blend of cultural experiprofoundlydeeply influences my writing, allowing me to weave together stories of personal growth, family dynamics, and resilience.

For aspiring writers, my advice is simple: Be true to your story. Writing authentically is the most powerful way to reach an audience, whether through poetry, fiction, or memoir. As I continue my journey as an author, I hope Petals of My Heart inspires readers to explore their own stories and emotions with honesty and courage.

Literary Deaths by Neglect?

Dan Ehl

I never thought that one day I would face the question – do I want to be a mass murderer and world destroyer? With the ninth fantasy novel in a series to be published in five months, do I want to begin the tenth? To not do so will mean the literary deaths of a cast of characters that now seem more real to me than some neighbors.

The humorous series deals with the exploits of Private Inquisitor Jak Barley and his supporting company of friends and citizens in the port city of Duburoake.

They began their lives when I first sat at my keyboard with only Jak and an opening scene in mind.

Through the real magic of imagination, one by one, beings like Jak's half-brother and alchemist, Olmsted Aunderthorn, came to life. Then followed the mysterious Lorenzo Spasm, a visitor from a world where magic does not exist, and spells hurled against him rebound upon the attacking witch or wizard. Morgana, a witch just finding her powers, entered his life in the second novel and became a key player in future cases. The list goes on, like Sergey Varvervane, publisher of The Weekly Tattler. Or Osyani hatched a harpy who became fully human following a blood transfusion from the nonmagical Lorenzo Spasm.

Through the more than 900,000 words written so far, I have come to learn the habits, frailties, loves, and fears of Jak and his friends. Since my writing is more like daydreaming and I never know what will happen next, I learned more about them with every book.

I mentioned my problem on a Facebook page for fantasy writers. Several replies said that using the same characters would make the stories tedious and formularized. I am still looking for that true.

So now I have to admit something. I have already answered my opening worry about becoming a mass murderer and world destroyer. They live. I am already halfway through the tenth.

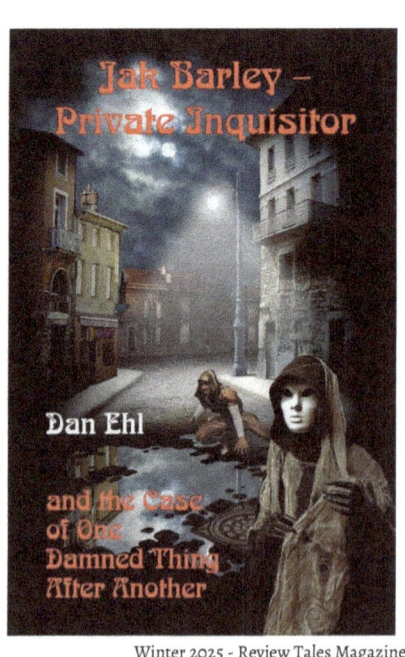

The Fine Line
Jenna Greene

As a writer of children's, middle grade, and YA, I'm often asked in interviews how I tackle dystopian realms and other severe topics for younger audiences and do so appropriately.

Good question.

I do so appropriately. I hope I do, at least. Writing for children and young adults is an essential and relevant undertaking. Often, a book is a person's first exposure to death, divorce, disability, and tragedy. I'm confident I'm not the only one who read "Bridge to Terabithia" or "Where the Red Fern Grows" and cried hysterically on their bedroom floor.

So, how would you like me to introduce these topics? Well, I don't shy away from the 'tough stuff'. I remain aware of the original purpose of fairy tales, knowing that showing harsh realities prepares children to deal with loss and adversity. They can encounter tragedy metaphorically in literature first, learning that the character managed a way to muddle through, as they will eventually do.

Of course, I know how I present specific issues matters. If I'm writing middle grade, and there is a death involved, I won't describe it graphically for pages on end. I'll tell it or not at all. It'll be a mention—a fact. Instead— of using detailed imagery, I will take the time to deal with all the emotions tied to the experience—the after. In writing for an older audience, I might describe death in more detail, but I will still make sure my characters are processing that loss. I might even hint at tragic events, having them happen 'off-camera' so those unprepared to understand certain concepts and events won't catch the meaning.

Children have rough lives. Sometimes, literature is an escape. It should be a wild adventure where they experience life and unknown worlds through vibrant characters. But literature must have a nugget of truth, no matter the genre.

The Proximity of Stars
by Benedict Stuart

When did you first realize you wanted to be a writer?

Funnily enough, when I was a kid, my dream was to be a writer.
I had no idea then what that meant. By all means, being a writer is hard work. There are no shortcuts or 'hacks'. Working smart is not precisely applicable here, unfortunately.
The reader will always sense that. However, the work is rewarding in many ways, not only financially. After all, the writer leaves something behind and gets to know various people, discusses different topics of interest, freely expresses personal opinions, etc.

How did you get your book published?

It was not easy, to be honest, but I am glad Next Chapter approved my manuscript after careful consideration. It is appropriate to say that this young and promising publishing company deserves praise. It is truly international and people-oriented and gives a chance to independent authors from all walks of life. The business model the company has created is innovative and modern. The community itself is remarkable.

Where did you get your information or idea for your book?

It sounds a bit banal, but real life is, in fact, an excellent source of ideas and inspiration. In other words, one's own experience could be a valuable contribution. We sometimes underestimate our uniqueness, including our life circumstances, personal growth, and the precious lessons we learn daily. Thus, sharing our thoughts, feelings, and understanding is enriching. Primarily via modern technology, allowing for worldwide coverage.

What do you like to do when you're not writing?

That is a good question. Most writers should have their day jobs - be sociable, active, communicative, and above all, inspiring others. Allegedly, with a good sense of humor as well.

As a child, what did you want to do when you grew up?

As I said, I wanted to be a writer, but I did not mean I would have only one job in the future. People nowadays must be flexible, versatile, and adaptable, keeping up with the latest developments in any professional area or pastime. As the saying goes, everyone has a book inside them.

TILL I Bleed No More
by Alexander Ellis

How did you schedule your life when you were writing?

At the time of writing, I didn't have much on due to COVID-19, so I selected timeless days, meaning I didn't have a set schedule and nothing else to worry about on that day. I wanted to spend at least 4-5 hours a day, roughly three times a week, writing, which mainly involved mornings and mid-afternoons. I would start writing at about 8:30 am and generally only write at night if it was some light editing; however, that changed in my third year of writing.

Where did you get your information or idea for your book?

My idea started with inspiration from a child I once knew in childcare in 2018. However, the idea for the protagonist of my book started with a Halloween costume I wore in 2016. I didn't mesh them together at first, but I started planning things in 2019 and then began actually to write in 2020. In terms of my information, I mostly searched the web but was also well-versed in pirates; most of my research came down to the ships at that time and some of the weapons used in the book. The plot itself, however, was my idea. I didn't draw it from anything, but in terms of worldbuilding, I borrowed much inspiration from Assassin's Creed Black Flag and the TV show Black Sails. Mutiny on the Bounty also inspired the ending of my novel; however, that wasn't originally my intention.

What was one of the most surprising things you learned in creating your book?

What surprised me most was how powerful this medium is; for the first time, I felt the strength behind an idea; it was like a possession, like a restless spirit inside a bottle that would rattle around if you tried to ignore it. I'd never felt like that before; I thought I NEEDED to complete this story because you'd be unable to rest if you didn't. I felt true belief as I delved deeper into creating this book. I was also surprised by how draining it is; you never honestly expect to know how much of a toll writing can take on you. I dried up nicely by the end of it, but to contribute just ONE great story to the World Library makes it worth it.

Is there anything you would like to confess about as an author?

I do not want to write many books as an author, as I believe in storytelling, that the power of the story is rare, and that quality is more important than quantity. It would be best to think honestly about your idea; only one of an author's stories can achieve this feat. For me, there's the story you can write, and then there's the one you should write. Another confession I would like to make is that I don't believe in a particular formula for stories; I know there are many techniques and theories concerning writing, but I'm not one of those authors who follow that.

Maestro! Maestro!
by Fred Calvert

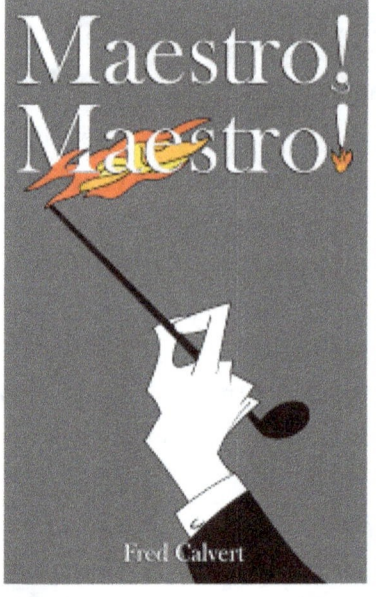

When did you first realize you wanted to be a writer?

In my early twenties, after enjoying so much great literature. Don Quixote was a book that urged me to pick up the pen.

How do you schedule your life when you're writing?

Early mornings are sacred to me. I do a ton of terrible writing, then. In the afternoons, I reduce it all down to okay ounces.

What would you say is your interesting writing quirk?

My imagination shuts down when it's too quiet.

How did you get your book published?
Self-published with Amazon.

Where did you get your information or idea for your book?
In the musical atmosphere of 'old Vienna' many years ago.

What do you like to do when you're not writing?
Walk and think about writing.

What was one of the most surprising things you learned in creating your book?

That it was allegory of my own life.

Is there anything you would like to confess about as an author?

My early life was a devil's deal. I escaped by writing.

As a child, what did you want to do when you grew up?

Be a singer.

How do you process and deal with negative book reviews?

With a ragdoll I stick pins in.

The Callum Walker Series
by J. M. Shaw

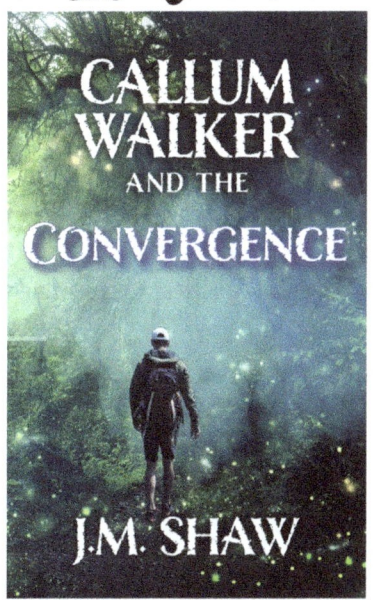

When did you first realize you wanted to be a writer?

I started writing thirty-two years ago because I needed a creative outlet. I loved making up stories, and since my mother had just bought me a typewriter, I tried my hand at writing. If I had to pinpoint the moment when I wanted to become a writer, that day, sitting at the dining room table, picking at the keys one by one, was that moment.

However, what started as a hobby soon became a passion and, eventually, an obsession. Now, I write because it's entertaining, a good stress relief, and emotional therapy all rolled into one, and I cannot imagine myself doing anything else.

How do you schedule your life when you're writing?

I am, first and foremost, a wife and mother. My husband and I have two busy boys demanding much of our time and attention.

While I spend as much quality time with my family, when everyone else is occupied, I slip away with my laptop to a quiet corner of our house and write as much as possible until someone notices me. I usually get about twenty to thirty minutes of creative musing before my kids start fighting or demanding snacks. Most of my writing happens on weekdays when my husband works and my kids are at school. I will typically rush through the housework and errands in the first hour or two so that nothing is left waiting when I finally sit at my desk.

Being that I have autism and ADHD, writing can quickly become hyperfocus, which is why I must set the alarm before I begin because I have been known to spend several hours working without realizing the passage of time. Once my children and husband return home, I typically put away my writing for the rest of the evening. Occasionally, I will try to work after my sons go to bed, but I often choose to relax.

What would you say is your interesting writing quirk?

I am not a planner. I have a solid idea of the beginning and end of each novel and approximately what needs to happen in the middle, but the rest is still being determined. I feel that this allows me the freedom to let my creative juices flow, and, at times, the story seems to write itself, and I'm just along for the ride. These moments of in-the-zone writing have often created scenes for which I receive the most compliments.

How did you get your book published?

I spent a few years trying to land an agent or publisher. While I had some offers, I turned them down because they all wanted to buy the rights to my stories and change some details. I could not bring myself to hand over the rights to my work any more than I could sell one of my children. The thought of changing my stories was no different than someone buying the "Mona Lisa" and drawing eyebrows on her. In the end, I decided to self-publish my work.

Nuggets of Hope, Cultivate Kindness by Kim Lengling

When did you first realize you wanted to be a writer?

I had never thought of becoming a writer. Years ago, I was asked to speak at a significant veteran event. I worked for weeks writing the speech, doing research, and conducting interviews. The day of the event arrived, and I stood before a large crowd of more than 800 people to give the speech. Newspaper editors and radio and television crews were also in attendance.

I was a bit nervous, but since the story I was about to share hit close to home, I took a deep breath and began to speak. Approximately 15 minutes later, I shared the last word of my speech, and the entire area was silent. I immediately thought I had bombed this speech.

But then there was one clap, another, and the crowd erupted. I realized I must have done an OK job sharing this personal story. Afterward, the local newspaper editor approached me and asked me if I would like to write a monthly column on veteran issues for the newspaper. His request surprised me, and I replied, "Oh, thank you so much, but I am not a writer."

He then asked me who had written my speech. And I replied, "Well, I did."

"Well, then you're a writer." was his reply.

At that moment, someone saw something in me that I had not noticed, and I began to think I could try this writing thing.

I wrote a monthly column for that newspaper for close to 14 years. During that time, other opportunities arose, and I continued writing. And now, all these years later, I am coordinating anthologies with other co-authors and creating and writing my books. It's been an exciting journey.

How do you schedule your life when you're writing?

About five years ago, I realized that if I wanted to write seriously, I needed to change my life. Once I decided to put more effort and more time into my writing and collaborative book efforts, I changed how my daily schedule played out.

As I work from home now, I can create a schedule that works for me. I put no stress on myself. That is a big part of it. I am placing no stress on myself and writing when I feel the urge to get writing. There are days I won't write anything, and then I write for hours. And you know what? Each instance is perfectly okay.

Apollo's Raven
by Linnea Tanner

What do you like to do when you're not writing?

I enjoy gardening, walking on the pathways near our house, and visiting with family and friends.

What was one of the most surprising things you learned in creating your book?

One of the fantastical abilities in Skull's Vengeance was inspired by my research that Celts believed the soul resides in the head. As with many aspects of the Celtic warrior's life, taking an opponent's head in battle, preferably in single combat, has a mystical significance. To possess the enemy's head is to maintain his soul. Skull's Vengeance explores the concept thatsupernaturall powers can be summoned from souls entrapped in their skulls. A shapeshifter and sorcerer, Catrin's half-brother conjures forces of nature from the skulls of family members he has slain to destroy his enemies in battle.

Is there anything you would like to confess about as an author?

Creating stories in my head has been a way for me to deal with challenges in my own life and career. When I admitted this quirk to a colleague, she gave me a look that normal adults don't have imaginary friends. Fortunately, I discovered that authors have childlike wonder and imagination. Memories, images, or news on the airways can trigger stories. Storytelling is used as a lens to view the world in different ways.

How do you process and deal with negative book reviews?

If there are any constructive suggestions, I'll consider them in my future writing. Since my books realistically depict brutality and mores of an ancient culture, a scene may trigger an adverse reaction. I've become aware of this and have thus tried to create book covers and excerpts that communicate the genre (historical fantasy), the themes, and the tone of my novels to appeal to my reader base.

As a child, what did you want to do when you grew up?

As a child, I wanted to be an actress, movie producer, or author.

One Hand Screaming: 20 Haunting Years by Mark Leslie

When did you first realize you wanted to be a writer?

My desire to be a writer might not have been with me as long as my desire to become a storyteller. As far back as I can remember, I loved creating stories—tales I would amuse myself with as a young child while playing with little Fisher Price action figures. For me, playtime wasn't just play; it was a chance to toil in an intense engagement of "what if" and imagine epic adventures I would conceive of for these little plastic figures.

Something extraordinary happened when I discovered the magic of transposing these story ideas onto a printed page. They were plucked from my imagination and mind and onto something that could be transferred for others to read and enjoy.

It started with my creation of little stick-figure cartoons and other drawings. As I got a bit older, I would write out longer tales, and in my early teens, after discovering my mother's Underwood typewriter on a shelf in her closet, I started typing those stories.

I typed up and submitted my first short story to a writing contest at fifteen. It was rejected. But I never gave up and kept writing new stories and sending them to various magazines and markets. After five years, hundreds of submissions, and almost as many rejections, I finally sold my first short story in 1990, which appeared in print two years later.

I never gave up and continued to make writing a significant part of my life.

How do you schedule your life when you're writing?

I had always made time to write for most of my life. Whether it was school, work, or family life, I had to make sure that I didn't just find the time but made the time to get my writing done. If I needed to get up at 7 AM to get ready to head to work on time, I would, for example, set my alarm for 5 AM and spend those first two hours of the morning writing. Or, when taking a commuter train from Hamilton to Toronto, Ontario, I would use that time each morning for several years to get writing done. I recall writing the first draft of a novel during my first year commuting to a job in Toronto. Since late 2017, when I left the corporate world and began focusing more on writing and doing part-time consulting about the writing and publishing business, my ability to ensure solid blocks of writing time became a lot easier. But I continue to do my best to get my serious writing done early in the morning—over the years, I have found that to be the best time of day when my creative juices are flowing.

However, nothing gets those creative juices flowing like a deadline. So, regardless of the time of day or what else is going on, if there is writing to be done, particularly to meet a deadline for a contract with a publisher or an editor, the important thing is to get my butt in a chair and my fingers on a keyboard.

The Girl Who Changed The World
by Machiel Hoek

When did you first realize you wanted to be a writer?

I didn't want to become a writer; at some point in my life, I had to become one. In 2013, an inner voice clearly instructed me to break free from the rat race and forsake the alluring promise of wealth that awaited me. This voice also resurfaced a childhood memory that left me feeling deeply inspired. At the tender age of six, I yearned to uncover the secrets of life—the answers to its grand "why" questions: Why does the world exist in its current state? Why is there so much suffering? Why am I here?

So, I had to embark on a quest to discover The Grand Secret of Life. And I promised myself and the world that if I discovered that Big Secret, I would share it in a compelling story that would adapt to the reader. Soon after that, I went to Burning Man in the Nevada Desert, where I experienced a life-changing moment. I virtually "met" Lisa, the daughter I always wished for but never had, and that faint spark turned into a blazing fire. Though she was never a real-life daughter, Lisa became the main character in my book and a vessel through which I uncovered one of life's most profound secrets. We embarked on a transformative journey together, and Lisa changed my world.

How do you schedule your life when you're writing?

I've never scheduled my life… When I'm writing, I try to plan my day or writing week, but the actual course of events always deviates from my planning. I learned that my best writing occurs when I don't plan, schedule, or anticipate anything and let myself go with the flow.

My biggest challenge was balancing writing with running a business and making time for my family. Writing felt like a "calling," which at times seemed selfish. Thankfully, my wife believed in my vision and sometimes even pushed me out the door, urging me to go somewhere and write with complete focus. Every writer needs that kind of support — someone who encourages you to take action, whether kicking you out of the house to write or just reminding you to stay focused on your craft.

How do you process and deal with negative book reviews?

Well, my wife is the biggest fan of my book, but not because she isn't critical of me – far from it! After reading the first manuscript, she said: "That's why I married you!".

Some two years ago; my book had been published for a few months and sales were finally picking up, I heard her screaming and shouting downstairs. I ran down to find out what had happened. She had just read the first negative review of my book, and she was furious, ab-so-lu-te-ly furious!

I laughed and tried to calm her down, explaining that no book is for everyone and that certain people will always dislike any book. And that's okay. Well, for her it wasn't. Until now, she will react with disbelief and fury to a negative review. And I will let it go.

She Called Me Throwaway
by Shama Shams

What inspired you to write "She Called Me Throwaway – a Memoir"?

My inspiration stems from the profound understanding that my experiences could serve as a guiding light for someone navigating deep despair and hopelessness. I can offer hope and practical tools for overcoming adversity by sharing my journey. Knowing that my story might resonate with others fuels my passion for helping them find strength within themselves and envision a brighter future. It's a reminder that no one is alone in their struggles; even the darkest moments can lead to transformative change. By connecting with others, I hope to ignite the spark of resilience and empower them to reclaim their narrative, turning pain into purpose.

Writing about personal trauma can be cathartic but also retraumatizing.

How did you navigate the emotional challenges of revisiting difficult periods?

Writing this book was a lengthy process that required countless hours of therapy and deep introspection. I carefully chose the specific details to share, considering their significance and the depth to which I wanted to explore them. Establishing boundaries was essential; I understood what I was comfortable revealing and what needed to remain private. This thoughtful approach allowed me to share my journey authentically while protecting my emotional well-being. Each word was a conscious decision, reflecting my desire to connect with others while honoring my healing journey.

What advice would you give to others who want to tell their stories but might be afraid to start or share them?

Writing your story is a profoundly personal journey that only you can navigate. It begins with a commitment to authenticity—embracing your unique voice and experiences. Remember that you can decide who gets to hear your story and how much you choose to share.

As you craft your narrative, think about the themes and moments that resonate most with you. What lessons have you learned? What struggles have shaped you? Could you consider the emotions you want to evoke in your readers, whether empathy, inspiration, or understanding?

Ultimately, this process is about your growth and healing. Your story can provide hope and connection for others navigating similar struggles. Embrace the journey, knowing that your voice is powerful and deserves to be heard.

The House Filler
by Tong Ge

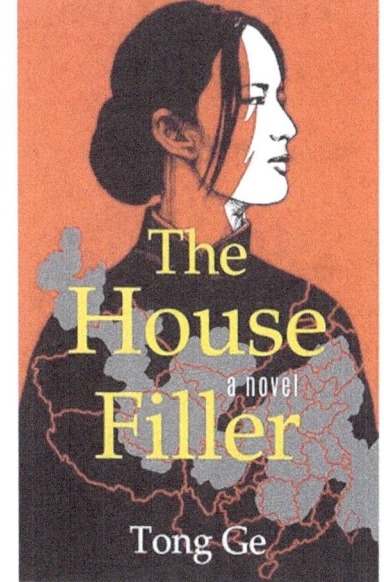

When did you first realize you wanted to be a writer?

I wanted to become a writer when I was in junior high. In China, we study Chinese from grade one through grade ten (there were only ten grades in my time), and we have had weekly writing assignments since grade four. The following week, the teacher would select two or three of the best pieces to read aloud to the class. My writing was always chosen. This early recognition gave me great confidence that I could become a writer one day.

How do you schedule your life when you're writing?

I've had a commission-based job since 2005, which gives me great flexibility in my working hours. For the first fifteen years, I would go to work between 10 and 11 in the morning, bring my lunch and dinner with me, and work until 9 PM. After that, I would start writing in the office until 11 PM, or sometimes until midnight or 1 AM. I call this time my "happy hour."

What was one of the most surprising thing you learned in creating your book?

The romance between my grandma and a young man 27 years her junior. In reality, they weren't related at all. He was just a boy from the street whom she occasionally hired to help out. After my grandpa passed away, this boy became a family member.

Where did you get your information or idea for your book?

"The House Filler" is based on my grandma's story.

What do you like to do when you're not writing?

I enjoy reading, going to live theater, swimming, traveling, volunteering, and learning new things.

To be a Fae Legend
by Tricia Copeland

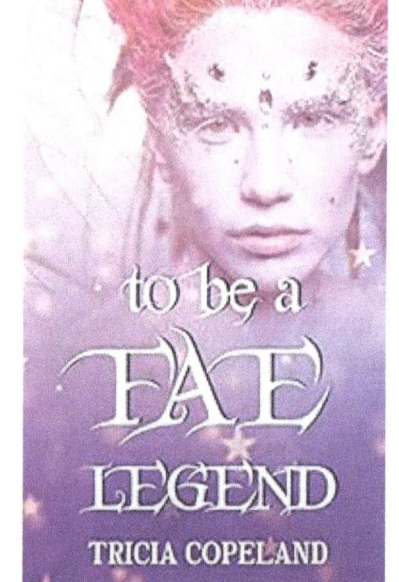

When did you first realize you wanted to be a writer?

My writing journey began with scientific writing as a graduate student. Before my master's program, writing was complex and daunting for me. A fantastic professor coached me through technical writing, and I realized I loved it. Fast forward twenty years, in the throws of raising three young kids, I started writing to entertain myself. This mini obsession became my first book series, Being Me, based on my experience with anorexia. That grew into a massive obsession with the paranormal and fantasy genres.

What would you say is your interesting writing quirk?

I'm not sure this is a writing quirk, but being a very visual person, I love maps and images of characters and settings around me when I'm writing. Sometimes, when writing and hitting a slow spot, I'll create a mock cover or browse for cover, scene, or character images. For my Realm Chronicles series, I have maps of my world printed out and next to me, as well as character lists and descriptions, so I can keep track of where my characters are, how they look, and how they act so I can ensure that I'm remaining true to each character, scene, and storyline.

Where did you get your information or idea for your book?

Information and ideas for my books come from many different places. For example, after publishing my first series, I wanted to write a fantasy book, specifically a vampire book. I was drawn to urban fantasy, a contemporary paranormal setting where the humans were unaware that vampires lived among them.

For the Kingdom Journals series, I created a character that is half vampire and half witch, a breed forbidden by both the witch and vampire communities. To add to her challenges, she's been mainstreamed into a human high school. I formed her history and path based on Christian histories, which led me to write a series primarily based on witches, specifically a trinity of mostly witch beings who must find each other to break a curse on the witch lines. Often, my ideas for books come from anthology invitations. My dystopian novel, Lovelock Ones, featuring two teens on a quest to save a sibling from a viral plague, grew out of a healing-themed anthology. My fae series, the Realm Chronicles, started with a short story for a fantasy anthology where the main fantasy character faced mental health challenges.

EDITING: YOU ARE YOUR OWN WORST ENEMY

J. L. Yarrow

Everyone loves my novel! Really? Could you define everyone? "Well, my family and my friends. They all left great reviews on Amazon." Anyone else? "Well, no, not yet."

Do you think that sounds familiar to you? My next question would be, who edited your work? "Ummm... my friends and family."

Have you heard that before? LOL... me too. Our family and friends mean well, but they're not trained editors. They see through rose-colored glasses because they love and want us to do well. Nothing wrong with that. So, who should edit our manuscripts? You can't rely on yourself to dig into the details. You're too close to your story. Your mind misses those tiny typos, etc. Trust me. I know. I have that same problem myself. When it involves editing, I am my own worst enemy.

Should you publish your work without a professional edit? Many writers do that when they go the self-publishing route. They have a lot of errors, typos, spelling, grammar, story inconsistencies, etc. If you've ever downloaded a free or 99-cent book, you know what I'm talking about.

I've read many of these books, most of which could be so much better if they'd gone through a professional editing process.

Interested? You can start by hiring a professional editor to do your line edit. That title needs to be more accurate. It focuses on your work at a line and paragraph level and reviews your writing style, content, sentence structure, etc.

And yes, put on your big boy/girl pants to work through a line edit. Some say you must have a thick skin because of the painstaking way the editor points out your shortcomings as a writer. I thought of it as a college course in my novel. I learned so much from it; more importantly, it helped make me a better writer.

IN ITALY - NOW AND THEN

Lara Gelya

I first visited Rome in early 1990, seeking a new life after escaping the Soviet Union. My citizenship was revoked, leaving me stateless as a "Refugee of the World." Despite my limited funds, Rome became a place of profound cultural discovery. I explored landmarks like Vatican City, the Colosseum, and the Trevi Fountain and had a life-changing interview at the American Embassy that permitted me to go to the U.S. In 2024, returning to Rome on a Mediterranean trip felt deeply nostalgic, reminding me of my journey and struggles.

Reflecting on my time in Italy in 1990, I recall my initial impression: I found Rome noisy, dirty, and chaotic, unlike the clean streets of Austria. Yet, Italy's warmth soon won me over. The language was musical, the bread unforgettable, and the people vibrant and lively.

In my first weeks, I stayed in a cold, unheated bungalow near Rome. Sick and weakened, I spent days by the seafront, recovering in the sun and sea air. Later, we moved to Torvaianica, a coastal town near Rome, where I shared a small apartment with "Misha," a young man from the Soviet Union. Unprepared for daily life, Misha relied on me for food and guidance, but after he squandered our grocery money, I decided to stop cooking for him. Soon, another woman joined us in the shared apartment.

I often traveled to Rome, sometimes by bus, but I usually embraced the freedom of exploring. Rome enchanted me with its historic sites and free museum days, where I immersed myself in its timeless beauty. Back in Torvaianica, I strolled the streets, indulging in the sights and sounds of Italian life. I would linger outside a bakery, mesmerized by the display of tagliatelle, biscotti, and other pastries. The kind baker once offered me a taste, likely noticing my frequent visits.

I mistakenly went to the wrong location when I received the long-awaited call for my second embassy interview. Desperate and teary-eyed on a Roman curb, an Italian taxi driver came to my rescue. Without enough money, I paid him with a cherished ring, my only valuable possession. Arriving just in time, I met with embassy officials, who permitted me to emigrate to the U.S. after a brief, friendly exchange.

Years later, I returned to Torvaianica. The quaint town and once-coveted shoe store were now familiar and ordinary. Yet, the memories of my transformative journey, the people, and Italy's indelible charm remain etched in my heart.

PRETTY UGLY

Jennifer Anne Gordon

Looking back, I can see now that my path was marked early on, destined by a love for the mysterious and the macabre. My name is Jennifer Anne Gordon—I'm a gothic horror novelist, dancer, and choreographer, but as a child, I was an awkward, pale kid with asthma and allergies, often confined indoors. My escape was reading. I tore through Nancy Drew's books in first grade and moved on to the darker world of Christopher Pike. His edgy tales of teens facing the deadly consequences of bad decisions made me feel like I was entering a cooler, more thrilling world.

My parents supported my reading habit, even promising to never say no to buying me a book. They had no idea what they were getting into. I quickly moved from Nancy Drew to Christopher Pike novels, enthralled by his edgy tales of morally ambiguous teenagers facing consequences for their actions. These books were full of characters getting into trouble—accidental deaths, dangerous dares—and I loved every moment. Reading them made me feel like I was venturing into a darker, more astonishing world that felt miles away from my Catholic school classmates.

When I was ten, my uncle came to stay with us, bringing a bit of mystery. He wore a jean jacket with Native American embroidery, smoked, and spoke French with my mom whenever they had secrets. Intrigued, I often snuck into his room. One day, I found a thick book with a cat on the cover—Pet Sematary by Stephen King. Hiding behind my Victorian dollhouse, I started reading, feeling like I'd unlocked a forbidden world.

From the first pages, I knew this wasn't a book for kids. It scared me to my core but also broke my heart. I was hooked on dark, tragic stories and wanted more. My trips to the bookstore with my mom turned into covert missions. I'd wander into the horror section, mesmerized by the covers, before being escorted back to the young adult shelves mostly lined with Sweet Valley High. While I enjoyed the drama of blond twins at high school parties, I craved something darker.

That summer, I found my solution at a local flea market where my mother hunted for clown figurines (an unsettling collection in its way). I discovered a table covered in "gothic" novels, each for a quarter. The covers featured terrified women and dark castles, and I was captivated. I showed my mom Conjure Wife, hoping she'd let me buy it. To my delight, she did. With three dollars in hand, I bought an armful, launching what I now think of as my "Gothic Summer."

Those books were filled with eerie atmospheres and suspense, though many were about things I couldn't fully understand—like the jealous "magic" of 1950s professors' wives in Conjure Wife. But I was drawn to these stories' tension, sadness, and occasional thrill of terror. Even at ten, I knew this was the kind of storytelling I loved.

A few years later, Flowers in the Attic cemented my fascination with dark, twisted tales. Almost every woman my age remembers Flowers in the Attic as a defining book that left a lasting impression. My love for the gothic evolved from that point, and today, as a writer, I aim to capture that haunting, emotional weight in my work. I've never shaken the allure of tragic and eerie stories—they've shaped me, always pulling me back into their shadows.

WHY DO WE WRITE?

Mike P

Have you ever asked yourself, "Why do I write?" If your answer is "yes," then I imagine you've already experienced that moment when you finish your manuscript, polish it, put everything together, finally gather the courage to put it out there… and receive little to no feedback. It sucks, I know.

If you choose self-publishing and aim to make a living from selling your writing, your plan only has two steps:

1. Write an actual manuscript (if you've done this already—congrats! You can cross off the most straightforward step).
2. Could you tell people they want to read your book? At this stage, your success depends solely on your marketing genius.

"But I'm a writer, not a marketer!" you might protest. Yes, you are! So, my friend, relax!

Here's a thought: millions of people play musical instruments without aiming to make a platinum record. Millions of people create paintings without expecting to get them into fancy museums. Why? Because they love it! Because art is calming! Because art is exciting! Art touches their souls, brings them peace, and makes them feel alive!

If you're trying to force out a few dry words only because you've imagined mountains of gold, please get a real job.

On the other hand, if you're passionate about writing, let it be so. Do it against all odds. Please do it for yourself! If you find recognition along the way—good for you—it's a nice bonus but never the ultimate goal of your journey!

My friend, there's only one correct answer to "Why do I write?"—and it is: "Because I love it!" If passion is what drives you, then onward it is! And whatever the future holds remains a mystery!

P.S. Never show your writing to anyone until it's edited! Not even to your dog!

KIN'S QUEST
Ron Root

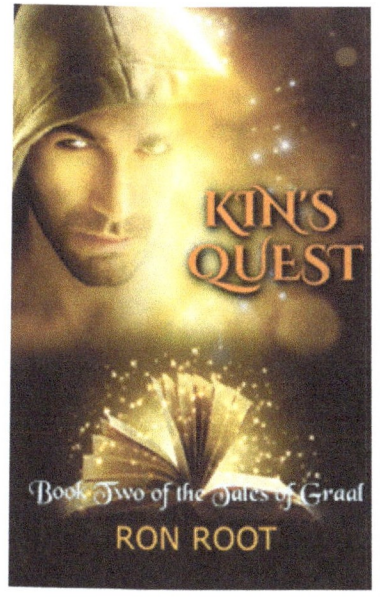

Writing novels has been a lifelong goal I've finally taken the time to pursue. Years ago, while flying from Oregon to Florida, I realized I had no book to read. Stopping in the airport bookstore, I bought a Terry Brooks fantasy novel and got lost in its story. So much so that a story of my own popped into my mind; it so haunted me that I put it into short story form. Then, over the years, it grew into a fully-fledged novel that became Nexus Moons, the first in my Tales of Graal series. Having read J. R. R. Tolkien's Lord of the Rings trilogy, I decided I needed to write at least two more. Kin's Quest is the follow-on novel that continues Nexus Moons' hero's saga. The third book in the series will continue the saga of characters introduced in the first two books.

Writing sci/fi fantasies offers challenges not faced with other genres. Given that the story world is fantastical, with which your readers are unfamiliar, the author must meticulously build it so it may be envisioned. The Tales of Graal is set in the equivalent of our own Middle Ages and, therefore, must accurately portray that period. Trickiest of all is language. Any modern word can jolt the reader out of the story. This forces the author to evaluate each word's etymology meticulously. Words in use before 1600 are my litmus. Like the other genres, the character arc must still be carefully honed, as does the overall story and chapter structure. Although work, it's a labor of love. Once done, a few things are more satisfying than learning that someone has read and enjoyed your creation. If you read this series, hopefully, the same can be said of you.

ODYSSEY OF HIGH HOPES: A MEMOIR OF ADVERSITY AND TRIUMPH
Cyrus A. Ansary

Reviewer: Jeyran Main

Cyrus A. Ansary's *Odyssey of High Hopes* is a captivating memoir that traverses continents and cultures, weaving an inspiring tale of resilience, ambition, and the pursuit of the American dream. Born in 1933 in Persia (now Iran), Ansary grew up in a world of tradition and family values. His memoir begins with vivid descriptions of life in Persia, offering readers a unique glimpse into his early years, shaped by a hardworking father who instilled in him the importance of education and entrepreneurship.

Ansary's journey from Iran to America is nothing short of remarkable. After earning top grades in school, he was chosen to join a group of students touring America. This experience ignited a desire in him to call the United States his permanent home, and with unrelenting determination, he saved up for a one-way ticket to start a new life in America. From living at the YMCA and working at a Montgomery Ward warehouse to earning a college scholarship, his story is a testament to the power of perseverance and hard work. Through sheer grit, he climbed the ranks of academia, ultimately becoming a Columbia Law School graduate, a U.S. Marine, and a highly successful entrepreneur.

In this memoir, Ansary also reflects on the history and cultural dynamics of both America and Iran. He recounts his encounters with various influential people and his contributions to his adopted country, which have impacted American society. His pride in becoming an American and his passion for giving back are evident throughout the narrative, making his story resonate as much with his gratitude as his achievements.

Chock-full of anecdotes infused with humor and insight, *Odyssey of High Hopes* is an exquisitely written account that captures the highs and lows of Ansary's journey. His resilience and determination will inspire readers, especially those who have dreamed of overcoming adversity to achieve their aspirations. Ansary's journey is a moving reminder of the strength it takes to carve out a new life while holding on to one's thoughts, and his love for America shines through every page.

For those seeking an uplifting memoir of triumph over adversity, *Odyssey of High Hopes* is an engaging read that illustrates the boundless potential of the human spirit and the universal yearning for a brighter future.

DECEPTIVE CALM
Patricia Skipper

Reviewer: Jeyran Main

Deceptive Calm by Patricia Skipper weaves a suspenseful and thought-provoking tale that delves into identity, societal expectations, and the far-reaching consequences of deception. Set against the volatile backdrop of martial law in South Carolina, the story follows Vanessa, a light-skinned Black woman whose life is shaped by a series of traumatic experiences in a Catholic orphanage. In a desperate bid to escape her circumstances, she assumes a new identity, using the birth certificate of a deceased white infant to reinvent herself. This bold act opens the door to a world of privilege and sets the stage for the novel's intricate exploration of race, class, and family secrets.

Vanessa's journey takes her to California, where she enters UC Berkeley and eventually marries into one of the state's wealthiest families. Initially, her life seems like a dream come true, but it all unravels when her child is born with sickle cell trait—a genetic marker that reveals her true heritage. Her ruthless and unforgiving husband feels betrayed and plots revenge, leading to events that thrust Vanessa's secret life into the spotlight.

Skipper masterfully constructs a suspenseful narrative, skillfully building tension as a young, inquisitive detective begins to unearth Vanessa's hidden past. What might have seemed like a straightforward case soon becomes a maze of lies, secrets, and cultural stigmas. The fallout threatens Vanessa's fragile new identity and shakes the foundations of San Francisco society, exposing the hypocrisy and prejudice lurking beneath its polished surface.

Deceptive Calm is a gripping novel that explores the devastating impact of racial identity manipulation in a world divided by appearance and ancestry. Patricia Skipper's writing brings these themes to life with vivid detail and emotional depth, making Vanessa's struggle relatable and thought-provoking. Through Vanessa's journey, Skipper invites readers to question the actual cost of survival and the lengths people will go to protect their own lives. This novel will resonate with anyone interested in stories challenging social norms and revealing the hidden struggles behind carefully constructed lives.

QUEST: FINDING FREDDIE: REFLECTIONS FROM THE OTHER SIDE

Thomas Richard Spradlin

Reviewer: Jeyran Main

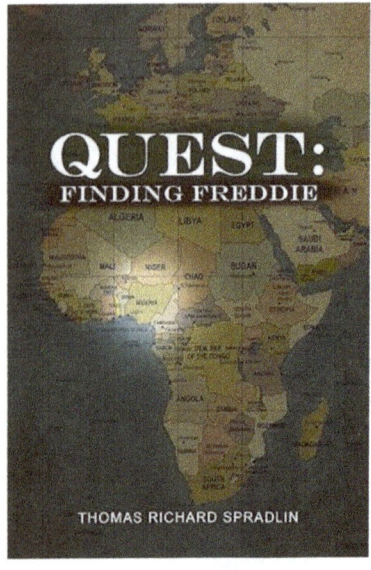

In *Quest: Finding Freddie: Reflections from the Other Side*, Thomas Richard Spradlin transports readers into a high-stakes search mission against the tense political landscape of 1970s Africa. This gripping narrative centers on the mysterious disappearance of "Freddie," a devout Jewish client of Spradlin's Washington, D.C., law firm, Clifford & Warnke. Freddie's sudden vanishing act on August 14, 1976, while on a business trip to Lagos, Nigeria, becomes the focus of Spradlin's journey as he sets out to locate him amid a volatile international backdrop.

Freddie's disappearance occurred just weeks after Israel's dramatic Entebbe rescue mission in Uganda, which left Ugandan President Idi Amin humiliated on the world stage. The region was in a delicate political state, with Nigeria itself reeling from an attempted military coup and the recent assassination of General Murtala Muhammed. Spradlin's account vividly captures the suspense of navigating these unstable conditions as he embarks on a personal and professional mission.

The book combines the elements of a legal thriller with the intensity of a political drama, giving readers insight into the complexities of international law, diplomatic relations, and the personal challenges faced by those caught amid political turmoil. Spradlin's background as a general partner at Clifford & Warnke lends authenticity to the narrative as he weaves his legal expertise and experiences in Nigeria. His reflections add a layer of introspection, making *Quest: Finding Freddie* more than just a story of mystery and suspense—it becomes a contemplation on loyalty, faith, and the lengths we go to help those in need.

Quest: Finding Freddie offers a compelling, thought-provoking read for those interested in historical dramas, legal investigations, and political intrigue. Spradlin's attention to historical context and personal stakes makes this book informative and engaging.

THE ADVENT OF TIME: A SOLUTION TO THE PROBLEM OF EVIL BASED ON THE PREREQUISITES OF LOVE
Indignus Servus

Reviewer: Jeyran Main

The Advent of Time by Indignus Servus tackles one of the most profound and enduring theological questions: If God is all-loving and all-powerful, why do evil and suffering exist? Taking a methodical, logic-driven approach, this book aims to provide a definitive answer to the problem of evil within the framework of Christian orthodoxy, addressing some of the thorniest theological challenges in a way that is intellectually rigorous yet accessible.

Central to the book's argument is that specific prerequisites—faith, free will, selflessness, and others—are necessary for a genuinely loving, reciprocal relationship with God to exist. These prerequisites, however, also open the door to the possibility of evil and suffering. The author argues that God's creation of "time" itself is intertwined with the fall of humanity, suggesting that time, as we experience it, came into being as a result of sin. This interpretation reconciles the biblical account of creation with evolutionary science, proposing that the progression of time and evolution reflect a fallen, time-bound reality, contrasting with the timeless, perfect state of pre-fallen humanity.

The book also dives into complex topics like the nature of hell, framing it within the prerequisites of love and the consequences of free will. Rather than offering a pastoral approach, the work is a theological treatise that aims to reconcile Christian doctrine with logic and scientific understanding. This thoughtful and concise exploration covers significant ground without overwhelming the reader, thanks to its precise, jargon-free style.

The accessibility of *The Advent of Time* makes it appealing to both lay readers and those more steeped in theological studies. Its arguments, rooted in the Catechism of the Catholic Church, are firmly grounded in Christian doctrine, offering a strictly orthodox perspective that might not satisfy all theological viewpoints but remains consistent with traditional Christian beliefs.

For readers interested in a structured, philosophical approach to the problem of evil that remains faithful to Christian orthodoxy, *The Advent of Time* provides a well-reasoned and unique perspective. It is an intellectual exploration of love, free will, and the nature of suffering in a world that often seems at odds with the idea of an all-loving God.

TOTEM BY CHARLIE SHELDON

A mining company has permits to extract erbium, a mineral that can detoxify coal, in the heart of Olympic National Park. Sarah Cooley and her companions want to return to Bear Valley in the Park one last time before mining begins. Carl Larsen, a retired wildlife biologist, investigates mysterious elk kills in the same area. A sudden windstorm upends everything just before mining employees, Sarah and her companions, and Carl converge on Bear Valley. Totem is the third and final stand-alone novel in the Strong Heart Series, tales filled with legend, magic realism, and ancient truth.

ADRIFT BY CHARLIE SHELDON

A container vessel catches fire in the Gulf of Alaska, forcing the crew to abandon the ship. One lifeboat crashes ashore on Haida Gwaii, off the British Columbia coast. The abandoned ship, adrift, becomes a salvage prize. Marooned sailors struggle to survive while relatives ashore become desperate—a down-and-out salvage tug races to seize the ship before the ship owner's tugs grab her first. Adrift, the second stand-alone novel in the Strong Heart Series, is a sea story of survival, courage, and the human spirit.